Sighing in Unison
presents

Golden Mean

when we surrender to the Seasons Creep
while we feed into our abnegation
viewing things through a myopic lens
not remembering
to have any humility
pearl clutching from fear mongering
but to them, that's only Murphy's Law
pine for a new start to be reborn
choose nature or nurture
and find your way
breaking out the ghost in the machine
return only upon meeting your noble
savage

red for the blood from death via greed
white representing the oppressive
blue as the feeling we experience everyday

obtuse is the thought of a world only using
your metaphorical noose
lurid is the grin
smug and stubborn
shedding seed in vain
immolating the next generation
with a gun loaded by gentrification

so similar, yet so different
between six degrees of separation

'golden mean'
by michael deabold

raindrops on oil-slick streets
a mirror of the city
beneath my feet
caressing my soul like silk sheets on my
bare body
my reflection calls out to me
blurry, undistinguished
yet undefeated
i can't decipher the message but i feel so
compelled
i walk forward, in parallel
am i outside or lost in mind?
losing track of time...

pieces of me lie tucked away
waiting to be released
you can't hide
from yourself
lying inside to get by but seeping from
the seams
it coils around me like a snake
taking my breath away
the fangs sink deeper into my flesh
but i continue on my path

the showers pick up
encompassing me
i look down to my feet, just for one
glance
a face appears; the person i crave to be
seeking my chances, i know what i need

there's a darkness that engrossed me
urges i can't fight, true to my being
unfamiliar territory, i tread bravely
footsteps washed away
i dissociate, disconnecting from reality
i lost my location, passed my destination

roaming deeper through the avenues
the streets are alive and i'm wilting
i find a bench and watch the passers-by
close the umbrella
fold my hands
and absorb the moment

he walks past me and locks eyes
i can feel him sensing, welcoming my duality
seductively, he whispers to me
something takes over, like a wave engulfing the
rocky shoreline
i can't deny him
nor break my gaze
i feel transparent
exposed

'exposed'
by hanna fierstein

you were building your spool
off of the roll
which i was unraveling from

by alex lisi

To meet someone clearly different from yourself;
of what true difference does it matter.
The true intent of heart is the wealth;
but silence, in response to that heart, does
shatter.

Your face, though of beauty, is merely
materialistic;
what presence of mind do you hold.
Does your heart follow a path to be
congenialistic;
or, of flesh and bone, are you truly cold.

I'm saddened by the fact that you did not try
to even attempt to overcome the shield
which envelopes the self that encircles your
mind;
and allow the forces of your shyness to yield.

If you were, in heart, taken aback by the sight
of the suddenness of me there, that you knew of
no words;
I forgive you in fact, but still is my plight;
the need for your words, in my heart still does
surge.

The thoughts in your head are succeeding the
face
which attracted me right from the start.
And if, at the moment, you feel that this pace
is too fast and shallow for the speed of your
heart.

Forgive me my sweet, but your beauty entails
what true essence therein lies in freedom;
but wait, in your avoidance, my heart lies
derailed;
as autumn changes colors; my soul out of season.

Please try in your youth to see how by chance,
my oure heart does qualify for your knowing.
Not merely for purpose of empty romance,
but with eagerness of truth to know you, I am
glowing.

I know, of my words, you have no mere
reference;
to follow the path of my future with zeal.
I seek your acquaintance; for your voice I hold
reverence;
the chance to reveal, in the flesh, I appeal.

Please swallow your pride and see to a meeting;
my heart does lie pure in this humble attempt.
I'm left with mere touch of our brief timely
greeting;
never knowing that on sight, I would become
exempt.

Your beauty and softness does sing through your
skin;
your eyes show what caring resides within your
soul;
for even the few words you espoused were
spread thin;
I know, is totality, of fine essence you are whole.

by joseph louis ravo

the city people are made of substance;
an allusion of disillusionment,
unrequited attention to the shadows.
mass exposés of cinematic noir.

'disillusionment'
by alexandra newman

a victim of a filthy mind
nuance and duality are a relic of the past
police gallows humor when it's not yours to
censor
an internet thread of what classifies
problematic behavior a little too wide
and i'm praying for a poignant intervention
that's divine
promise you'll consecrate the future
honeypotted to the point of self-abuse
licking your lips at the thought of capital
punishment
light the gas until i'm permanently un-moored
holding hands, we are cellmates
until the end
jovial of what's to come

sitting in this hell
having a staring contest

'esoteric'
by michael deabold

So, as expressions of hate lie hidden beneath
facades of goodness,
instincts of heartfelt forgiveness, may renew
your stale aloofness.
True meaning of "love your enemy," need not
be to turn your cheek;
Responding through emotion is the weakness
he does seek.

A mirror of reflection, absorbs not, of what it
sees;
The image, though detected, is allowed, at
once, to flee.
The moods you entertain in life are not your
own mind's planning,
they may be caused by a strife of your
manipulated handling.

Your willingness to respond as though a
puppet to each reaction
of your enemy's total construction to rule his
satisfaction;
to remain as calm in your center means
abstention of perturbance;
Allow no thoughts of anger to upset through
mere observance.

To lure you from concentration of previous contemplation,
is permitting satiation of your enemy's consideration.
Not responding, as though not there, attempts of mere distraction
will discourage future acts of hate preventing interaction.
As cause and effect can merge as one; they initially were one-sided;
But to realize well that your task be done- with your enemy you're united.

'freedom'
by joseph louis ravo

we were all in love
we were all in love with the sweet sound of
silence that existed and breathed and burped up
ideas and conversations and arguments and
and and and and .....
we were all in love.

i carried twenty-one like a bullet in my chest
like all of their hearts on my plate, in my belly,
all for me.

i love people for the first time
i love people for the first time
i loved people for the first time

we drove somewhere to get nowhere after
leaving a parking lot of laundry and apologies.
or something like that ...

we drove and i was safe with angels in the
backseat.

sometimes we fall in love and everyone after
can only pretend to understand
but they really don't

i knew them by the crook of their jaw
they knew me by the lace of my shoe

saw my eyes glaze over
heard my anger rot
twisted my arm back
we battled

like children do
knock the elbows
kick the teeth in

sigh in deep
and heavy
all at once

we love anyway

by christa ferry

we are VHS kids
eyes red from smoke and watching films play
the couch has our imprints
from staying up too late
Bogart ad Bond on the screen
we can't tell the meaning
so we break down the scene

covered in sugar and fast food
time is paused only for us
twenty-somethings, who cares
age doesn't exist down in the basement

watching problematic clips featuring Looney
Tunes
cereal bowls full and we can't find the spoons
old memorabilia reflects in the room
the sun is almost up
I think I have to go soon

Static is playing in our tired heads
I guess we're sleeping in tomorrow
Don't forget to rewind the tape
And then we will do it all over again

'VCR'
by michael deabold

every ounce of me
poured into you
i can no longer pour
what i do not have

by alex lisi

it rains and my petals overflow
the prick of a thorn, my thirst grows
the breeze tickles my leaves and warms me
but the sun is dim here, it's empty
around me the tree trunks are rigid
filled with tumors and lacking life
the ground blanketed in pine
how have I managed to survive?

by hanna fierstein

like cobwebs
sitting.
watching.
hanging around
while life moves around them
with no choice
but to watch

by alex lisi

Blind sighted as you decided, determined, the
rewrite the past and the future.
There was no ill intent with my touch.
I was not side-stepping the thorns, but
finding stable ground to grow my ivy.
Slow, even, overtaking the environment
around it.
You complained that I was everywhere.

Vitality required balance, and you were
always one foot out.
Whispering sweet words to a sapling does not
n=motivate or encourage growth,
but still, I waited for sweet honey to spill from
your mouth.

The love I fertilized for myself was always my
consolation prize for the love you could not,
and refused, to return to me.
I had dimmed my own sun
Poisoned my own waters
To provide these things for you, instead
Approached you with cold hands and placed
the tools to build your own shield
Taller in each open, panting palm.

Now, with an empty armory, I can offer
nothing
But a broken apology to the person you
helped create.

by brittny marino

i was just a vessel
in which for you to grow your future

by alex lisi

i feel stupid for thinking you'd say it back
i feel stupid for thinking this is different from
your past
that i'm different from the rest

i knew the risk i was taking
but i was not prepare for the heartbreak

i always fall for the emotionally unavailable
man
that is incapable of loving me back
or showing me the same respect that i deserve
that i earned
but i haven't learned from the cycle
that i wasn't meant to have a title

brick by brick and piece by piece
i take on these projects
i should be focused on myself and my priorities
instead of filling my head with silly love stories
that aren't life
the image is a lie i feed on to fill the need that
he won't

was any of this real?
or did i fall for the mirage in his facade
that the others had fallen for too?
have we all felt this pain in our chest
that comes with the awakening of knowing
you're all alone?

'where do i go from here?'
by hanna fierstein

my dreams seem macabre in nature
i get high on my melancholic solitude
thinking about the people I used to know
now y=look who' pregnant, married, or dead
melodramatic, i know, but that's just how i cope

we just got it started but we're already done
promise you'll stop blaming me for why you feel
disconnected

no matter how much i try
i can't seem to shuffle my mind
walking the line with you
only leads to me paying a hefty mental fine

i know you're tired of my corrosively caustic attitude
i've just been stuck in the teeth of people's astute
obloquy
conviviality went straight out the window
along with what's left of my dignity
missing the days when you would fawn uncontrollably
you can call me selfish

i'm just not doing well

i'm less than a ghost to you
i tried to send an olive branch
the postage stamp must have dried out
i've been alone for far too long
my devil-may-care mind is tweaking heavily
you handed me a shovel
to dig up the grave beneath
now i'm oversleeping under how much you truly
meant to me

'greyrocked'
by michael deabold and bryan j mangam

the rain races across my window like the salt-
laced tears that stream down my cheek
i plead for some insight but the silence is bleak

he said we can't be friends

but what have i done to deserve the cold
shoulder?
i carried his weight and hardship like a boulder
over my head, arms folding beneath it
but when i was at my lowest, he took my misery
and toyed with it like a child

all i'm left with is the dust of the memories of
what was and what could have been
i still wear the necklace he bought me for
Christmas
because i can't let go of Him

why does it hurt so deeply to cut the chord all
over again?
i've been through this before, i should know;
i wasn't prepared for this

over the last year you've put me on a
rollercoaster
with no way off the ride
i'm ready to jump off at this point
some days it feels like i'm going to die

i know leaving you was the right decision
you couldn't keep your word
and stick to our commitment

all of the hiding brought me back to childhood
searching for the need;
playing hide and seek
finding a knife piercing at your heart
betrayal was a theme from the start
trust was a pipe dream and i am a sleeper
sleeping beauty' he was my keeper

'sleeping beauty'
by hanna fierstein

Televangelists on television stations passing on false salvation
News outlets pleasure themselves to views exploiting cancellation
Fall for buzzwords in headlines of Buzzfeed based in reductionism
Holding a pitchfork listening to NPR salivating
Demonstrably false infomercials are condescending
Fallacious ideals blocking out iconoclastic thinking
Social codes but only in the ire of the beholders diner plate
What's there to say when it could be half my age plus eight?
Superficially seductive in a cyber age of reproduction
Sniffing up a line of a narcissistic supply of validation

Omission of guilt is just another fabrication
Fake apogies of misogynistic values and internalized racism
Sexual repression via non-consensual circumcision
Rough fornication brainwashed off of pornication
Dehumanization through the kaleidoscope of objectification
Gerrymandering to the point of banned abortion
Solipsism at attempts of bon viviant gratification
When in reality it's just more mental masturbation
Sitting at home high playing your PlayStation
While Ukrainian and Palestinian citizens fear their annihilation
When it's time for a call of duty you always seem to be missing

Western kids grow up and are told, "aim for the stars,"
But never reach their high school graduation
Billionaires flying high in the air crashing right into a foreign child's education
ICE separating families with their unjustifiable deportation
Liquid funds flowing through pipes unless you live in Flint Michigan
What once was pure now suffers from defloration
Leading to a fix off the street to a vein giving numbing elation
Can't afford a yellow paper with a doctor's prescription
Support systems not universally covered ends in self medication

The sun burns bright on the future generations
Antinatalists hope for the end of human population
Darwin looking down at what we call civilization
God sighting at what we molded in ode to his creation
A business man in Japan wearing a tie around his neck
Supported from a tree of the giving
Outside an overworked factory makes little importation
He'll hope for a new tranquil like through reincarnation

'ostrich trap'
by michael deabold

i asked you what you wanted
you listed three things
none of them were me

by alex lisi

BEST WISHES

always smile!
PONY BROWN

keep in mind.

I'll always know

ne places you go

3:33 p.m.

I want

something stronger

in its purest form

everything i am
everything i used to be
does not coexist
as if always in battle
and i'm the one who suffers

by alex lisi

I always believed in forgiveness
But slowly losing sanity and patience
Lately I can't help but feel impetuous
Chattering teeth from frustration
You're crazy if you thought I'd let you paint me
out with black
Motivation to prove you wrong returns back

you always seem to drag down the flag we both
put up
I'd climb Mount everest to keep you away from it
When your mind finally breaks you'll see true
meaning and purpose

As you dig a hole to Hell I can't afford to wait
Because once you enter its gates there's nothing
left to create
When there's nothing left to say
Feel the flames at your feet from you having it
your way

Are you proud of what you've done?
Have you finally learned this isn't always
supposed to be fun?

You can't relate to the responsibility and pride
that comes with the duty
You'll eventually learn bitterness tastes sweeter
with a feel good story

'don't worry, it's just business'
by michael deabold

checker mark tragedies
line up for the daily routine
patterns of limitations set the normality
he is me and we are they; faces of the gray
time melts down the walls
Big Brother rules it all
a free mind is dangerous in a world boxed in
blurring boundaries between insanity and what
we live
look in the mirror, what do you see?
a free spirit? or what they tell you to be?
lie to me to make me blind
the ignorance is bliss because truth is hard to
find
a mirage is the comfort zone, cover your eyes
feed me the poison; the pink slime
what is real? what is fake?
genetically mutated and presented in vain
have we truly been animalistic or humane?
tamed to be the same, camouflaged chains
alien to a materialistic world with no reflection
the affliction feeds the addiction to remain
identical
you have the power to open your eyes
but would you choose to see?

held down by "the man's" tight leash
i want you to run and think free
would the world be what it could be?
a color is eveything but what we see
is peace a dream or a necessity?
tell me who to be; i'll bow down and kiss your
feet
put the money in my wallet, the food in my
mouth to eat
a slave to the economy, capital reigning
supreme
corruption bleeds through the screens
washed to hate, what to love and believe
wake up from your slumber; see that you've
been deceived
bend your world around you
things are not always as they seem
what is a true grasp on reality?
where is a code of ethics being set on our
morality?
ripping away from savagery
hypocritically civilized but truly slaves in
different chains
will you choose to change or remain the same?
in the checker-board world boxed in gray

'checker mark tragedies'
by hanna fierstein

you appeared in my life the same way your face appears in my phone every night -
a light disturbing the darkness, brightening everything in its path.

the only difference is i've come to expect these calls every night, but i certainly didn't expect you to pop up. lately, you've had a habit of making things better.

you made winter warm, with hugs like hot choclate and kisses like the snowflakes that fell from the sky every week for months in Connecticut.
you made meals alone feel like family dinners, recipes including a pinch of stories from your day and a heaping tablespoon of comforting words, with extra chipotle mayo on the side, always.

you made nights away from home into sleepovers with old friends, falling asleep before the movie was over and giggling into cheap fleece blankets way past bedtime.

no day together was just another day- it was a memory.

and that's something i wasn't used to, growing up in a please where some days were battles and others were wars.
where my armor was a Jansport backpack and a sweatshirt from Hot topic.
where my only weapon was sinking into bed, hours early with headphones on, where this fight had no end in sight-

my whole life, every night, i just needed a light.

and then here you are, shining brighter than every lamp in the library, glistening like the grass on the quad on the first warm day of spring semester.
and suddenly, everything feels so simple.

suddenly, i don't have to be everything that everyone wants me to be. i don't have to be the gorilla glue holding the family name together, the daughter pretending that she doesn't cry when she's all alone at the end of the day. i don't have to be the Cool Girl who's okay with everything and bothered by nothing and would practically shapeshift to be the kind of person that some kid from Vermont's frat brothers would approve of,

Ii don't have to be the friend who's *so good* at taking jokes and *so secure* in herself and can totally handle being told she's the least normal person who went to high school and would never be taken home to meet somebody's parents.
i just have to be me.

me, who can unclench my jaw, relax my shoulders, and take a deep breath.

me, who doesn't have to laugh when someone's roommate makes a joke that isn't funny.

me, whose even-year-old self finally feels free to laugh and play and explore; to make mistakes and still have everything be okay.

to play mermaids and princesses and fairies, to cuddle up and fall asleep with no fears of anybody leaving.

perhaps the light in the darkness was more than a light; it was a key finally finding a way to open a door that didn't even have a lock saying, "it's okay. you're here, you're safe now. you don't have to fight anymore."

'a light in the darkness'
by jennifer moglia

The moment it all connected
Every cell in my body unanimous
Knowing what would come next
I can't do this anymore
Then came the pain
Relentless waves of sadness
Storms of self-doubt crashing down
Thunderous clouds of shame, failure

Breathe in, out

Finally, the tides subside
Tears evaporate, taking this weight with them
Stress drained out of me almost instantly
Revealing the best part of the process

'the rebuild'
by alex lisi

Dreams are like
Mysterious lovers
Dangling in between
Fate's grasp and
Ardor's gaze.

You are an inamorato vision
Hidden behind eyelids
And poised fingertips

Asleep.

'inamorato'
by alexandra newman

as the night howls and the wind blows, i am
letting go
letting go of the pain as i slip away
away from your grasp, you hold no power over
me
you are no more than a memory
i've spent months trying to wrap my head
around the reality

there's no rhyme, reason or morality
i didn't deserve this, where did you find the
audacity?
i never thought you could steep so low
i fill my cup until it overflows
i release all sorrow in order to grow
"you reap what you sow.

as above; so below, i am letting go
no more falling down the rabbit hole
no dwelling on the answers only you know
in the darkness, your true colors show

i let go of the anger, fear and dread
i'm no longer hanging by my last thread
i'm no longer the woman you misled
i'm done spending my days crying in bed
lock you out of my head- all focus on me
instead.

'letting go'
by hanna fierstein

the birth of venus, a lover.
beauty to hold, but her hands are shaky.
sex, lust, charm. is that all that is to be seen?
on the surface, perhaps.

venus, a planet; earth's sister.
second to the sun, second to most.
she is bright, brighter than the stars
themselves yet her light dims in comparison.

she gives so much of herself to the sky,
immeasurable warmth.
even the sun is jealous.
but then wonders why she feels so empty.
uninhabitable by her own doing; maybe too
warm.

beauty, they say, a word that holds too little
value in a world of infinite beauty.
lonely in her place; no moons to keep her
company.
for she would rather make hell for home
if it meant sharing warmth with another.

'ode to venus'
by jackie volta

Eight years in the making
Like a shot in the head
and Abe Lincoln's dead
Check on your multitudes
It's time to share the wealth
Now, cheers to my health
Oh, the heart is on display
They call me Tax Day

It's a long damn island
Been a real hard damn year
And I am their multineer
On horizon, iceberg
The maiden voyage failed
Sometimes we prevail
Oh, the heart is on display
They call me Tax Day

He's what we waited for
So much still in store
He's what we waited for
So much still in store

Oh, the heart is on display
They call me Tax Day

'tax day'
by bitters and distractions

As I remember how my father would sit
Beneath the large oak tree;
And I would manicure its giant limbs,
as he wished accordingly.
"A little off, over here and there,"
He would say after much consideration,
"Let the sun shine through the limbs;"
As I proceeded with my mutilation.
I kept in mind my mom's instruction,
Not to let too much sun shine through.
In fear he would burn on his knees and
face,
As the sun would shift in the afternoon.

I loved that big old oak tree for how it gave
him a safe haven to relax;
And how it provided the shade that be
As he sat and dreamt with a shawl on his
lap.
He would sit and listen to his tiny radio, of
insignificant this and that;
As my mom would travel to and fro
To check for whatever he would lack.

And as the years did pass too fast,
And the pieces I trimmed would just grow
back;
I was grateful for the time that passed
And for these simple favors I could pay him
back.

by joseph louis ravo

You used to be so safe and kind
Now I question where you put your time
Ever-changing is this world
But never thought it would be my girl

All I want you to admit is that you didn't love me
As much as you thought you did
Maybe this is all a phase
Maybe this is permanent
A lot went by since we last spoke
It's been awhile since we put our names in the proverbial
wet cement
Those letters no longer exist on the pavement

My head is a movie theater playing our time together
I'm living with your former self's ghost
Who projects a reel of memories of when we loved each
other most

Went to sleep without answering your call
And slept until I had a dream of running through the
ceremonies hall
Now you're married with two kids
Happily living post escape from my quicksand

House bright red
Lawn envious green
Starting right back at me
Maybe if I stare hard enough it'll go up in flames

I'm too stubborn to be all the way happy for you
But I'll do my best
As you plant a garden wearing a yellow sundress
Dedicate a blue flower in my name
From the soil, I'll watch over you
Petals spin in the wind
Hoping they grow somewhere they can live

'two different people'
by michael deabold

Callous is my heart, as the wood of mighty oak.
Dry is my soul, as the ever sodden desert.
Silent is my tongue, since mere words seek no
path.
Blind are my eyes to life's pain.

Soil rich earth fed of flowering fields;
Decomposed once living matter yields new life.
Things of true value surpass what is naught;
In spiritual growth is no strife,

Sustained is the cry for superbial riches;
Suppressed are the yearnings of true warmth.
Not heard are the moans of the crushed and the
weak,
As thr courage to survive fades from strong.

Fire in my eyes once glittered like spark,
As well as in heart and in mind.
Not fearing what life could erode from my heart;
Not caring what my future would find.

Though since life has stolen my true love of old,
The meaning of joy now escapes me.
My grasp of simple pleasures too weak to
behold;
What was once held and enjoyed inately.

Now lifeless as well as a sleeping old oak,
Awaiting new life from its source.
Shielded from love; thick bark as its cloak;
Seeking love to revitalize remorse.

by joseph louis ravo

Oh but will you be bored
of beauty
and grand vistas
that bleed over endless horizons?

When the last wave breaks
and the last sun sets
on your last breaths
will you be bored?

Of laughter and applause,
which will fill your head
with grand ideas of no death,

The bones in your body and whites of your
eyes
and time gone by
in passing.

That sickness unto life
is death,
and the dizzying angst of daily contention

And halcyon days
you're pulled from
until you've seen more sunsets
than you will ever see again.

But it is a serious thing,
Oliver said, to be alive
on this fresh morning in a broken world.

Do not turn away.
Do not adjust your set.
You won't be dull,
for it's the end.

Watch the trees,
their lushness rising,
for it's the end.

'halcyon'
by b. john gully

Golden hour does exist
inside of our close,
the lucent finish.

A climax of pastel shades
Rising,

And setting.

The mating of the fade
and sky.

'the fade'
by alexandra newman

How close can you come to eternity?

The Contributors
(In Alphabetical Order)

Michael Deabold
Bitters and Distractions
Christa Ferry
Hanna Fierstein
B. John Gully
Alex Lisi
Bryan J Mangam
Brittny Marino
Jennifer Moglia
Alexandra Newman
Joseph Louis Ravo
Jackie Volta

Executive Editors
Bryan J Mangam
Michael Deabold
Sam Espinoza
Melissa Kristen

Edited By
Sam Espinoza

Art Direction By
Bryan J Mangam
Michael Deabold

Cover Art By
Lena Espinoza

Interior Art By
Nysa Ciliento

Published By
Sighing In Unison
I'm Just Here
Productions
Water The Soil